THE POW

INFINITY
SYMBOL

Working with the Lemniscate
for Ultimate Harmony
and Balance

Barbara Heider-Rauter

EARTHDANCER

AN INNER TRADITIONS IMPRINT

First edition 2018

Barbara Heider-Rauter
The power of the infinity symbol – Working with the Lemniscate for Ultimate Harmony and Balance

This English edition © 2018 Earthdancer GmbH
English translation © 2017 JMS books LLP
Editing by JMS books LLP (www.jmseditorial.com)
Originally published as *Die Kraft der liegenden Acht: Mit der Lemniskate zu unendlicher Harmonie*

World © 2016 Schirner Verlag Publishers, Darmstadt, Germany

Cover design: Murat Karaçay, Schirner,
Cover illustration: Calmara/shutterstock.com
Layout: Anke Brunn, Schirner
Typesetting: Dragon Design UK
Typeset in Minion
Printed and bound in China
ISBN 978-1-84409-752-4

Published by Earthdancer, an imprint of Inner Traditions
www.earthdancerbooks.com, www.innertraditions.com

Contents

4   A short exercise to get started

Before I tell you more about the infinity symbol, its spiritual meaning and the many ways in which you can use it, I would like you to do a short exercise – it will help you to experience directly the wonderful energy of a symbol that can connect you with the most positive things in life.

All you need are a length of cord, or several pieces of cloth that you can knot together to make a rope, and a companion to assist. There is no need to arrange the room in which you're going to do the exercise in any particular way, and the whole thing will only take a few minutes. Place the cord or cloth rope on the floor in the shape of a closed circle; it should be big enough for both you and your companion to fit inside comfortably.

Stand within the circle, facing one another. There's no need to think of anything in particular, just both be aware of how you are feeling; you might feel perfectly happy, or perhaps a little constrained – all kinds of emotions are possible. The exercise is not about evaluating or analysing, it's simply about being aware, so be as relaxed as possible. When you are both ready, step out of the circle. Now rearrange the cord or rope on the floor in the shape of a figure-of-eight

and step into it, one person in each loop, standing opposite one another. Just explore your emotions – you will probably both be feeling freer and more at ease in the loops of the figure-of-eight, while also being able to feel the harmonious energy of your mutual connection. Feel how the energy of the infinity symbol begins to pulse and flow between and around you, in an endless stream. The vibrations of the eight swing from one side to the other, always crossing through the stable centre point that links the two loops.

This constant flow of energy creates a deep connection between two people – a union, although neither has any influence on the other. Both have their own space and are able to retain their unique identity, yet both are linked through a deep relationship. This exercise demonstrates the importance of the infinity symbol to us; it links two different energies to form a harmonious whole. They are able to retain their own individuality while becoming part of each other or recognising the other as a harmonious part of themselves.

Swap experiences at the end of the exercise and try it with as many people as you can persuade to take part – you will feel this boundless balancing and harmonising energy

6   each time. It teaches us how an inner connection can also be made in complete freedom, and we learn this not just with the analytical left half of the brain but also with the right half, the emotional brain.

Introduction

We live in a society in which we communicate only partly through language; we are often unconsciously influenced by symbols as well – a self-contained world that affects us daily. Our world is generally ruled by symbols, which have much more effect on our subconscious than we could imagine, so it is not surprising that knowledge of the subtle power of symbols was jealously guarded in the past, to be used by the ruling classes and passed on as secret knowledge.

Nowadays we are fortunate in that much of the old wisdom has become available to everyone once again, and we all have the chance to use these powerful signs and symbols to assist us on our own path towards a more conscious living – a positive development both for ourselves and for others. Many recognise the symbols, but very few are aware of their effect upon us. Symbols are used both singly, in isolation, and combined to form logos used in advertising, for business cards and on everyday products. They have just one goal: to exert an influence in a given direction. Master the language of symbols and you will be able to recognise them and understand their meaning. It is up to us to go through life attentively, recognising and interpreting symbols and their messages – then we too can make use of this 'language'. The more consciously we perceive the hidden power of symbols, the easier we will find it to invoke their magic influence, or to escape it when necessary.

I have devoted myself to the study of the power and the use of symbols for many years now; this exploration of the infinity symbol is intended to gently guide you and help you open your eyes as you go through life, to attain a better understanding of the message of symbols. We will encounter many symbols that are used positively, and some less so. Every symbol has both capabilities – the negative is usually found by inverting or reversing the positive symbol. Taking the infinity symbol or lemniscate as a positive example, I hope that this small book will awaken your curiosity and joy in the language of symbols. The lemniscate is one of the few that cannot be reversed or inverted. We will learn to use its amazing balancing power for our own well-being and discover how to do the same with other symbols.

The lemniscate can bring great benefits to humans and all living creatures. Simple and perfect, it can be used at any time and in any place. It helps us to find our harmony and to achieve equilibrium on every level. The infinity symbol enables us to strike a balance in the polarities and duality that make up our lives on Earth. We can use it to appreciate and further the eternity of our continual personal development. I would like to pass on my own experiences with this powerful symbol in the pages that follow; I make no claims to absolute knowledge or perfection, I would just like to share with you the simple exercises and insights that have come to me during my many years of leading seminars, in the hope that they will be of use to you. Thanks to our imagination, the infinity symbol is easily visualised, drawn or arranged wherever balance needs to be introduced. Use this powerful symbol for personal benefit and spiritual growth. Use it to approach problems in relationships in a balanced way, to recover the flow of your energy and to restore yourself – to become more balanced and to make decisions more easily. You can achieve all this in a light-hearted way using the infinity symbol.

The lemniscate is a symbol of the eternal, but it is also a symbol of duality and all that is polarised here on Earth. It contains within it the ambivalences of the masculine and feminine, of what is above and below, of yin and yang, of within and without. From the moment we are conceived, we experience a polarised world. We experience separation at a very early age, and the distinction between Me and You, as we become aware of things that are 'Not-Me'. During our years of education as children, we form opinions and learn to distinguish between good and evil, right and wrong. We begin to analyse at an early age, recognising the duality in our everyday lives that exists in many things. We learn to make decisions and to say 'yes' and 'no' – yes and no belong together, neither possible without the other. When we say yes to something, we know that in so doing, we are deciding in favour of something and yet also against something else. This unity forms a whole, and recognising its holistic nature in turn brings us to our own unity, and a new wholeness and health. The infinity symbol contains within it an opportunity to explore this unity or wholeness, and to initiate wholeness and healing within us. The vibrations of the infinity symbol have a frequency that stimulates this wholeness and helps it to develop – so the more often we investigate these vibrations, the more beneficial it is for the balance of the polarities within us. The lemniscate helps us balance the scales of duality and find harmony.

The infinity symbol as an expression of our attitude to life

When we wear certain symbols, we reveal our beliefs and convictions or express membership of a particular group. We can also communicate our attitudes using a range of symbols. Or we may wish to use them (in the form of ener-

getic jewellery, for example) to activate something within or around us, something we know to be in our best interests.

We might wear items of jewellery decorated with the infinity symbol to balance our energies or to activate a particular aspect of our lives. This ancient symbol of perfection, balance, harmony and eternity is integrated into lovely pieces worn around our necks or wrists, on our ears or fingers, or in our hair. Giving a family member or friend this symbol as a gift is a beautiful expression of eternal love. Jewellery can be engraved with a description of whatever we wish to activate in the vibrations of eternity, whatever we wish to cause to flow. For example, the word 'love' works with our own energetic field on an endless, positive vibrational frequency as soon as we connect it with the lemniscate and apply it, while a tattoo would be the perfect option for those keen to have a permanent reminder of the power of the lemniscate. To acquire greater inner and outer wealth, write these precise words in the loops of the infinity symbol. More than one word can be placed within the loops at any one time.

The vibrations of the symbol will bring movement, balance and eternity to whatever is important to you. It is wonderful to receive the gift of a bracelet with 'friendship' engraved within a lemniscate from your best friend, for example, or a

ring from your significant other bearing the symbol and the words 'unconditional love'. If you are not feeling well, wear an infinity symbol with the word 'health'. If you (or loved ones) are about to take a difficult exam, inscribe the words 'knowledge' and 'wisdom' inside the symbol. Simply write within the loops all the things you want to bring into balance. The advantage of jewellery is that there is no need to keep reminding yourself of the particular issue. The infinity symbol has an effect on your skin, and thus deep within you as well, via your energy field. While you wear the jewellery, this balancing impulse will be transmitted to your energy field, which will change as it acquires greater balance. The same applies to decorations in a room or the lemniscate drawn on your skin with body paint or an item of clothing bearing the symbol. Whichever way you wish to bring the balancing energy of the infinity symbol into your life, the key is to actually do it and to enjoy it.

Only recently, I came across an event I interpreted as a sign that people are once again becoming aware of the infinity symbol. A renowned theatre company in a large city had dedicated its dance and ballet programme to the 'eternal loop', including no fewer than eight different interpretations by eight different choreographers involving performance pieces based on the 'sideways eight'. I thought it was both wonderful and absolutely unique.

The performances were sold out long in advance, in itself a sign of the extent to which humans can intuitively sense the positive effects of this vibrational frequency. Just imagine how fantastic it is for hundreds of people to spend a whole evening visualising the energy of the infinity symbol and enjoying its balancing effect. For me, just knowing that eight individual choreographers had put together a programme in harmonious cooperation shows the direction in which this new society can develop, and the uniting power the balancing energy of this potent symbol. Even during the ballet company's rehearsals, the vibrational frequency will have been broadcast from the studio across the city, inter-weaving the eternal vibrating energy of harmony into the city's energy field, day after day, linking worlds and preparing the path for a new way of being together.

This raises the hope in my heart that the wonderful gifts left behind for us by our wise ancestors and an enlightened priesthood will find their way to us.

The lemniscate symbol

We are all familiar with the figure eight and how it is written. The infinity symbol looks like a horizontal eight, an eight placed on its side. It consists of closed loops symbolising the absolute and the eternal, with neither beginning nor end. The symbol contains within itself eternal motion, and so represents continual development and the equilibrium of all dualities. It is also known as a 'lemniscate', a term coined by the Swiss mathematician Jacob Bernoulli in the 17th century. We can use this symbol to bring everything into healthy balance. For me, it is one of the great keys to opening up a new society – if we wish to find our balance and re-establish a harmonious way of life, we will also have an opportunity to create harmony and equilibrium around us. Finding our way from the extremes of too much or too little towards harmony, making the adjustment from over-emphasis to balance, are just some of the things we can start to do by using the infinity symbol.

The continual development that we can support with the infinity symbol enables us to follow the path of enlightenment, to balance the forces within us and to experience fulfilment in our existence. No longer will we experience duality as a burden, and the balancing of duality and harmony will allow this Earth to become the paradise it can be. We will recognise that there will always be duality in our earthly existence; paradoxically, this knowledge will relax the tension within us and allow us to experience harmony.

The infinity symbol in different cultures

The infinity symbol crops up repeatedly in a huge range of cultures as a symbol of eternity or as a snake. A serpent with a body shaped like a lemniscate guards the path that leads back to unity and healing. The band adorning the forehead

of Egyptian pharaohs was thus decorated with the body of a snake in the shape of a figure eight. Snakes and the lemniscate also occur in Indian cultures – in representations of kundalini energy, for example. Kundalini is the energy that must be awakened on our earthly journey towards enlightenment. According to tantric teaching, it is the life force that rests symbolically at the base of the spine like two coiled serpents.

The infinity symbol also appears in Hermes' staff. The serpent associated with the Fall of Man and banishment from Paradise can now help us find our way back to unity. It shows us the importance of placing our energies in the service of the higher divine plan. It is a healing helper, enabling us to come back from what divides us and return to what unites us, to serving others. It helps us to leave behind tendencies to be manipulative and instead find our way towards the forces of balance and the recognition of polarity; this is why we hold in our hands the key to experiencing the energies of peace and harmony on Earth. We can see within ourselves much more clearly using the energy of the snake; it leads us repeatedly into temptation to demonstrate the spiritual development we have attained as it tests our resilience, our sincerity and our truthfulness, our understanding and unconditional love, our patience and the wisdom in our lives.

Once we have learned from our original encounters with duality and achieved unity ourselves, we no longer need fear the snake – it becomes a protector of our eternal development, bringing health and salvation, a steward of the wisdom of the infinity symbol and a guardian of the divine creator's plan, and of its magic. It is therefore not surprising that the symbol created by linking the serpent and the infinity sign has so frequently been used as a sign of power by rulers and across every culture.

From a spiritual point of view, eight is the number of the Initiate, one who has gone through the seven stages of enlightenment and crossed the seven heavens. Eight is also the number linked with the power of resurrection and regeneration. It symbolises the power of bliss, and of paradise regained. It is regarded as an imperial number – the Imperial Crown, the crown of the kings and emperors of the Holy Roman Empire, is octagonal in shape, and many imperial buildings similarly follow an eight-sided floor plan.

In Egypt, the figure eight occurs not only in the jewellery adorning the forehead of the pharaoh but also as the number of Thoth, the god of the Laws, of wisdom and magic and of the sciences (especially mathematics and astronomy). The Greeks related Thoth to the god Hermes. He is considered

the creator of geometry and numbers. He is one of the guardians of the gates to the realm of the dead, noting every deed of each soul wishing to cross the river into the underworld. At the entrance to the world of the dead, the crimes commited by each soul are weighed against the feather of truth. In Christianity, the baptismal font, which symbolically represents rebirth, is often eight-sided and some chapels and churches have an octagonal floorplan. There are also eight Beatitudes, and both the Old and New Testaments of the Bible teach that eight people survived the Great Flood.

Buddhists follow the eight-fold path to spiritual enlightenment and there are eight auspicious symbols, each representing an aspect of Buddhist teaching. In different cultures, we encounter eight suns, the day is divided into eight sections, there are eight regions of the world and eight chakras; an 8 x 8 shape represents the order of heaven created on Earth and Hindu temples are based on 8 x 8 symbology. In Islam, we find that on Judgement Day, eight angels will bear the throne of Allah, which encompasses the world. These correspond to the divisions of space and the eight groups of letters in the Arabic alphabet. In Japan, there are eight gods in heaven and in Japanese the number eight is also used to mean 'many' in the context of 'an indefinite number'. In the Jewish Kabbala tradition, eight represents perfect intelligence.

Eight means 'perfection' and is the numeric value of IHWH or YHWH ($10+5+6+5 = 26, 2+6 = 8$) and so is considered the 'Number of the Lord'. The Temple of the Lord was consecrated on the eighth day. The number eight and its special meaning also occurs with the Ancient Greeks, e.g. Plato, who said that eight celestial spheres of different colours surrounded the shining pillar of the heavens. And according to Pythagoras, the energy of the figure eight represented stability.

Hermes' staff

Hermes was the messenger of the Greek gods; it was his task to take messages to and fro between humans and the divine. In Roman mythology, he was known as Mercury, and the caduceus (staff) carried by Hermes and Mercury is thus identical, but should not be confused with the staff of Asclepius, the Greco-Roman god of medicine. His has only one serpent twisting its body around a wooden stick, whereas Hermes' staff has two snakes winding their bodies up around it in eternal figures-of-eight. At the top of the staff, where two large pairs of wings are attached, the heads of the two serpents stare into one another's eyes.

Hermes' staff is a symbol of the unification of male and female energy, or of opposites, rising up together from the earthly plane in harmonious balance and turning to the heavenly and divine in union with one another.

Much like the staff of Asclepius, Hermes' staff is used as a symbol for healing. However, while Asclepius' staff expresses a single aspect – only one snake winds its way up – Hermes' staff represents wholeness and the incorporation of body and spirit (or soul). The two serpents also symbolise duality, masculine and feminine, and the wings stand for the divine. Hermes' staff thus represents the peaceful and harmonious energy of equilibrium and coexistence. When the two snakes oscillate together in harmonious motion, union with the divine is achieved.

The works of the Bulgarian philosopher Omraam Mikhaël Aïvanhov feature very precise descriptions of the ascending paths of the two snakes and how these are linked with our path towards enlightenment as humans. Aïvanhov maps the snakes of Hermes' staff onto our bodies as a chart to explain the possibilities of using this symbol to awaken ourselves. Its symbolic power lies in turn in the realisation that unity, wholeness or indeed healing can be brought about through the unification of seeming oppositions. In order to make use of the message of Hermes' staff for ourselves, we must understand that it is all about bringing new balance to antithetical elements. Only then will we create inner harmony or wholeness in every area of our lives. The eternal motion within the infinity symbol, i.e. the coils of the snake around the staff, demonstrate to us that everything is always in flux, moving from one pole to the other in search of balancing harmony, with a view to creating unity.

Through the tradition of his symbol as it has been handed down, Hermes, the messenger of the gods, shows us that the eternal potential of the creator's flame lies within equilibrium. By overcoming earthly illusions, we create the union of heaven and earth within us, and thus also around us. Hermes' staff is well-known as a symbol of tradespeople, and in ancient times was also used to denote heralds, granting them diplomatic immunity.

The lemniscate – a mathematical symbol

We also find the symbol in science, specifically in mathematics, where the lemniscate is used as a symbol for the concept of infinity. In 1655, the mathematician John Wallis became the first to use it to represent infinitely large amounts. In science, the symbol enables quotients that could not otherwise be described to be classified and calculated.

Number pyramid

This number pyramid should help you have a better grasp of what I am saying and of the magic of the number eight.

$$1 \times 8 + 1 = 9$$
$$12 \times 8 + 2 = 98$$
$$123 \times 8 + 3 = 987$$
$$1234 \times 8 + 4 = 9876$$
$$12345 \times 8 + 5 = 98765$$
$$123456 \times 8 + 6 = 987654$$
$$1234567 \times 8 + 7 = 9876543$$
$$12345678 \times 8 + 8 = 98765432$$
$$123456789 \times 8 + 9 = 987654321$$

The Moebius strip

The Moebius strip is often shown as a sideways eight, although it is not a lemniscate – it is a three-dimensional object rather than a two-dimensional symbol like the infinity symbol. The Moebius strip can be defined as a surface that has only one side and one boundary.

It is named after the Leipzig mathematician and astronomer August Ferdinand Möbius, who described it in 1858, coincidentally at the same time as (but independently of)

the Göttingen mathematician Johann Benedict Listing. The Moebius strip cannot be oriented; it is impossible to distinguish between top and bottom, inside and outside. If you were to start colouring in one side, by the time you had finished, both sides of the entire strip would be covered.

What is the significance for us and for using the infinity symbol in our everyday lives? Symbols contain the energy that they represent. When we use different symbols, we send out a call to the energy field that surrounds us, which will send back an appropriate answer. The infinite nature of the lemniscate can greatly benefit our personal development – emotionally, cognitively, physically and spiritually. We experience ourselves as eternal beings, possessing infinite means of expressing our individuality. Duality is perceived not as a limitation of our potential but as a favourable element of our endless capacity for growth, inhabiting the creative power within us.

In the lemniscate, we have a means of achieving a balance that helps us achieve greater control of our lives. We progress from exclusion to acceptance and towards harmonisation, which in turn promotes our infinte potential for development. The lemniscate represents the infinite number of gifts that our lives have in store for us. Using this symbol regularly will therefore help us to grow into the creative beings that we truly are. We understand that the true power of humanity lies in acceptance, integration and harmonious balance.

The eight in numerology

The numcrological significance of the number eight is of course also contained within the infinity symbol. Following on from the sacred number seven, said to carry the energy of the mystics, eight also includes an understanding of the interplay of the visible and invisible worlds and an intro-duction to the magical interconnectedness of all existence. When we learn to look beyond our limiting spirit, when we break free from the constraints of the behavioural patterns we have been taught and release ourselves from our earthly bonds, we will be able to immerse ourselves in a world of endless opportunity and unlimited growth.

The eight is perfect in and of itself, infinite, without begin-ning or end. It bears endless love within it, infinite peace, unbounded progress for everything we can possibly imagine. In geometry, the concept of eight is represented with an octagon; the octagon bridges the gap between the rigid angles of the square, a shape that is more limiting still, and the infinite circle that knows no beginning and no end. The figure eight is represented by two circles that meet at a point.

For me, the fact that the number eight also has associations with the people of Atlantis is very significant; those who survived the sinking of the city and its destruction styled themselves 'the Eights'. Working on the premise that there was a highly developed culture in Atlantis and that, at its height, every being within it had achieved enlightenment and a deep sense of connectedness, we can see why the priests and priestesses were at pains to save the wisdom of Atlantis for a new era. If we make the link between these ancient spiritual riches and our own age, we become aware that the number eight has an even greater significance and symbolism associated with the lemniscate than perhaps previously thought.

The balancing flow of the lemniscate helps us to appreciate the mystery of our lives. Whenever we see or use the symbol, we are reminded of the ancient, infinite wisdom of the 'path to enlightenment' known from the marriage ceremonies of Atlantis. Our cells begin to vibrate and resonate with the information contained within the symbol and guide us towards an enlightened life.

The number eight helps us not only to comprehend the eternal cycles of life – death and rebirth – but also to feel their vibrations deep in every individual cell. The more deeply we are reconciled with these cycles and the more easily we accept them, the more our lives will flow. Once we have integrated this knowledge into our fundamental beings and aligned all our actions with it accordingly, there will be nothing left for us to struggle against. The path of our earthly incarnation will be all the more enlightened – and also simpler. The wise priests and priestesses of Atlantis wished to leave us a simple sign, the means to understand that the way to escape the earthly ties of duality lies not in passing judgement on separating polarities but in combining opposites to create a new unity.

Once we understand this infinite wisdom, we will find the peace we long for within us. We will be able to relax and love every form of life on the planet equally. Healing will take place within us and around us. Each division means death, as those who divide the world destroy it. Transforming destruction into unity is achieved through making connections and balancing opposites. A new society will be created from the transformation of divisive thoughts and actions into the energy of unification, as represented by the figure eight and the lemniscate.

The number eight also represents the mercy of eternal life and perfect cosmic equilibrium. The centre is at rest, but around the centre there exists an eternal flow of life. The spirit enters the material world, understands its laws and constraints, overcomes them and goes beyond the point of complete stagnation in order to return once again to the ancient continuum. All material consists of light and vibration. Light can superimpose itself onto light, creating a shadow, but when light outshines light, all that ultimately remains is light. We can block the light from our lives, but we can never remove vibration from our lives, because everything is vibration. Everything that surrounds us, and everything within us as well, is vibrating and in motion. We might even say that, in a certain way, all material 'shines'.

The world is a magic mirror containing all the possibilities open to us. Depending on our perspective and level of personal growth, however, it only allows us to see what we are ready to understand. The entire Earth is ruled by the law of polarity and our whole existence is informed by it – it represents the sphere of learning and duty for the souls and spirits of every being. Only in the centre of the source of creation is there no polarity, and when we are there, we will experience the perfection of absolute wholeness. The number eight represents the flow of life towards this wholeness. It represents both complete harmony and the creation of something immortal, something that will outlast our lifetimes across many generations. It helps us to clear the clutter from our hearts and focus on joy and ease, rather than experiencing everything as heavy and stagnating. The infinity symbol helps us to recognise new directions. The scales fall from our eyes and suddenly we see the world around us with a heightened consciousness. We begin to understand that we can start afresh each day, that our opportunities are endless and that we can grow and progress daily.

The number eight teaches us to be mindful of ourselves and all the living things around us, and to be mindful of what our hearts quietly tell us. The number eight enables us to be mindful in all our encounters, thoughts and actions, and to develop mindfulness in our speech, a powerful instrument of creative power. The number eight helps us to remain curious about new experiences, to see the flow of life in constant renewal, and to follow its path without fear but with joy at all the new directions we can take. The number eight keeps us in motion and gives us an inner harmony that continues to emanate from us constantly, permeating the world around us. It promotes within us a harmonious relationship with our surroundings and makes us aware of the forces that connect us. It allows us to develop an understanding of polarity, of the Other and of the Unknown, and promotes peaceful solutions.

In numerology, eight is also the number of architects, of builders, of painters and of all those who wish to create something lasting – just as the priests and priestesses of Atlantis wanted to create something that would be true for ever. We are the builders of a new world, a new place to live on planet Earth that is to endure for us and for those who come after us. Our experiences of Atlantis should always remind us that we are here to create this new world in a spirit of togetherness, of balance, of perfect unity.

The infinity symbol in the tarot pack

In a time when simply passing on knowledge of the interconnectedness of all beings was forbidden (as the mighty rulers did not allow people to be independent, free or empowered), wise people discovered how to preserve the universal wisdom in such a way that it remained accessible but could only be interpreted by the initiated. The tarot was created to reveal to mankind the truth of universal laws, the magic of all existence, of all that is, and the interconnectedness of the cosmos and to bring us closer to our true creative power.

These sacred symbols are found in the images of the tarot. For centuries, the old knowledge bided its time, waiting patiently for an era in which mankind would want to awaken and use this ancient wisdom for enlightenment. For people who learn to read and use the tarot correctly, it provides an inexhaustible source of wisdom that can lead us along the path of initiation to inner perfection. It is a great tool for all those embarking on the search for universal wisdom and the interconnectedness of all things – a discipline for self-exploration and development/working towards a conscious life.

But what does the tarot have to do with the infinity symbol? The lemniscate is also found in the ancient riches handed down in the symbols of the tarot, especially in three key cards that relate to our earthly existence and our potential for development. Nowadays, there are plenty of decorative and artistic versions of the cards and a wide range of tarot decks is available, but some artists have not adopted the old symbols as well. However, the cards in the 'Rider-Waite' tarot and the 'Aura-Soma' tarot use the original symbols and signs.

The lemniscate occurs in the Major Arcana on the Magician card, which has the number 'one'. In the illustration, the Magician is shown with the lemniscate above the centre of his head. Deceptively simple, the symbol holds the entire wisdom of the plan on Earth within it. It shows us that there is a desire, buried deep within the plan for our souls, to find our way back to unity or one-ness by recognising the infinite potential for development that we find in duality and in the correct balancing of that duality.

The Magician reveals to us our true capacity for creation and indicates that we carry within us the power of change. We can make use of these capacities according to our level of development. The tools are neutral in themselves; the Magician indicates whether they are used for the benefit of all living things or for their manipulation. Our purpose in our earthly incarnation is to follow the path of life and of unconditional love. We learn not to judge or negate duality, but to balance it out – this creates wholeness and healing within us. The infinity symbol helps us to connect opposites and to bring a new order and loving acceptance to the whole spectrum of earthly existence within us. The Magician shows us how important it is for us here on Earth to focus particularly on those things that link and balance us. By accepting and owning the duality within us we become whole again, and

activate the powers available to us on this planet to change our surroundings. We become wise magicians ourselves.

The second card in the tarot that shows the lemniscate is the Two of Cups in the Minor Arcana. This card is the second crucial key and an extremely useful guide to how we can bring our earthly journey to perfection. The Cups symbolically represent our emotions and feelings. The card bears the number two, the number of yearning for connection, of duality, of polarity and of the realisation that a peaceful Us can only be achieved through acceptance of You. The Two of Cups, with the lemniscate acting as a link in the image, shows that the key lies in recognising all our feelings and then bringing them into balance. The infinite nature of our feelings may help or hinder our path to enlightenment. Once we learn to bring our emotions into balance with the infinity symbol, we shall once again become creators of a new world. Our emotions represent the greatest hurdle on the path to full awakening, to conscious being and to enlightenment. When we are ready to embrace the duality within us and to accept the communion of the male and female aspects within us, we shall have achieved our full creative power.

I do not want you to read these lines, nodding your head in agreement and thinking 'yes, that's right, I knew that anyway', but instead would like you to think about why you are not yet ready to accept your less noble emotions – how do you feel about those thoughts and feelings of envy, jealousy, rage, anger, hatred, laziness, inadequacy? How do you deal with them? Do you see them as a disruptive element, as something with which to do battle, as a failure on the path of spiritual awakening? Or do you just accept things as they are, calmly examining why they are the way they are and what you can do to integrate your feelings into the situation?

How happy we are to recognise what we perceive as our good emotions, like love, joy, understanding, sympathy, peace – and how often we judge ourselves harshly when our less noble emotions get the upper hand. In seminars, I often see how participants are almost ashamed when they think about any supposedly bad or dark feelings they may have – they try to resist the emotions, then chastise themselves with self-judgement and self-condemnation. However, the lemniscate is a simple way to help us to recognise the polarities in us in this world as a given – the way things are. We must not allow ourselves to become 'bogged down' in these negative feelings or thoughts, but instead bring our emotions into balance and change for the good everything that might stand in the way of our growth. The Two of Cups card shows the connecting of opposites – all our feelings are a part of us and each is justified; they are a mirror of our inner sensibilities.

The third card featuring the lemniscate is called Strength and is also part of the Major Arcana. It is numbered eight and depicts a woman gently opening the mouth of a lion with her bare hands – with the lemniscate hovering over her crown chakra. This is another indication (for those who wish to learn) that we have the strength and the courage to live our lives in harmony in the way we have always wanted to – when we unite the male and female energy within us, for example. Emotions and rationality need not be at odds with one another but can work together to help us achieve a harmonious and balanced whole. We are so fortunate that, in the form of these three Tarot cards featuring the infinity symbol, the medieval masters left us a sign guiding us towards the path to perfection by accepting and balancing our duality.

By learning to reconcile ourselves with the laws of the Earth and gaining a profound understanding of the duality that always surrounds us, from the moment of our conception to when we pass on from this Earth, we have the opportunity to give our lives a completely new direction. Using the exercises with the infinity symbol, we can restore our strength and creative power and use our energetic resources wisely and for the benefit of all living creatures. We can leave behind our emotional dramas and become creative, happy and rich within ourselves. The key to achieving this lies in the infinite capacity for growth and development deep within us that we learn to use by recognising the duality and perpetual motion of the infinity symbol.

For me, the fact that you can use the lemniscate and understand the profound teaching of the universal wisdom the symbol can bring is quite brilliant – so simple and yet so comprehensive.

The significance of the number eight for the Chinese

In Chinese, the word for the number eight is 'ba' and its pronunciation is very similar to 'fa' (meaning 'wealth' or 'fortune'), so it is regarded as an auspicious number that brings happiness. Eight is so important to the Chinese that the Olympic Games were opened in Beijing at exactly 08:08 on 08.08.2008.

The Chinese tradition of feng shui includes the balancing energy of the eight trigrams, a useful guide for the harmonious arrangement of our living and work spaces. The ancient wisdom of feng shui is a real treasure trove of knowledge concerning the harmony of all beings. In China, you will find any number of banks, commercial enterprises and state or public sector buildings – not to mention private houses and apartments – that have been planned, built and decorated after extensive consultation with a feng shui master. Just as it is perfectly normal practice in traditional Chinese medicine to view a person as a whole, as a unity of body, spirit and soul, it is also commonplace when designing one's everyday surroundings to create the most harmonious flow of energy or chi possible. Life energy is perceived in balance and not in

isolation. The eight different areas or trigrams are brought into conjunction with the people who occupy these spaces; the aim of all feng shui is to establish the greatest possible balance between people and their environments. Here, the number eight emphasises that life is about happiness, harmony and prosperity.

In China, you will see many representations of the so-called 'Eight Immortals', eight wise people each possessing a unique talent. They will all live forever and cooperate with one another for the good of all those who ask for their help. Each of the eight uses his or her particular talent to achieve something extraordinary: the ancient sources tell us that they crossed the sea without any means of transport such as a ship or a boat, merely by having faith in the strength of their talents.

Humans have always been fascinated by the concepts of the infinity of time and space – the Eight Immortals are a mystical expression of the notion that time does not really exist and yet something akin to infinity is real.

The eight trigrams – and therefore the energy of the number eight – are also found in the *I Ching* (the Book of Changes). The wisdom of the *I Ching* is a useful tool for the whole of our lives and, much like the tarot, it offers the opportunity to achieve a better understanding of the connection between Heaven and Earth and all things physical. The *I Ching* was bequeathed by the wise ones of the ancient world in order to initiate us into the mysteries of life. The number eight is also found (and indeed is inescapable) in the truly ancient martial arts – many of which include moves that incorporate partial figures-of-eight and use the eight shape to lead into the next manoeuvre. The figure eight is closely connected with life and death, since every move in a combat may sustain life or bring death. Watch the movements carried out in contemporary tai chi, qi gong, karate or kung fu and you will soon detect the use of the eight shape. The ancient martial arts always involve bringing both the left and right sides of the brain into play and/or coordinating the left and right sides of the body. Hands and feet are never trained in isolation – the focus is always on wholeness and using the entirety of the fighter's potential.

Neutrality rises above the interplay of emotions and so leads to true power and creativity. The monks of the Shaolin Temple spend their entire lives practising ancient martial arts, not to fight an enemy but to achieve inner balance. Their goal is to strengthen and balance the energy of the infinity symbol within them and to focus on achieving a perfect state of silence and centredness and therefore the highest level of mindfulness. This alignment then allows them to work towards achieving perfect harmony, balancing left and right, top and bottom, within and without… giving rise to a capacity for exceptional feats of body and mind that seem to transcend the laws of gravity and astound those privileged to witness them practising martial arts.

Our infinite capacity for growth

When we use the infinity symbol, such as wearing it as jewellery or arranging it in different places, we open ourselves up to a new and harmonious way of accessing all that life has to offer. The lemniscate provides us with the power of infinity and helps us to achieve inner balance and harmony.

We are ready to explore an infinite number of possible solutions and therefore an infinite number of new directions. We recognise all the endless opportunities that are available and become more flexible in our thoughts and actions. We begin to believe that anything is possible. This inner balance and harmony allows us to appreciate the new directions open to us and to focus on the essential.

Using the infinity symbol activates the potential within us that otherwise may lie dormant, giving us greater access to our natural talents and resources. When we strengthen our core being and discover the path towards natural harmony, achieving balance becomes easier. We can tap into the vast resource of potential energy that is freed up, after which anything is possible. Only those who are entirely at peace at their core and can rely on the power of the collected golden energy at their centre, where the two sides of the vibration of the figure eight meet, can move the mountains of legend.

Exercise: Make your own lemniscate

Make a personal lemniscate containing everything you desire in your life. All you need is cardboard, drawing paper, coloured pens, glue and a pair of scissors. Begin by listing all the things you want to write on the lemniscate. Make it an appropriate size, one that will activate and/or harmonise with a wall in your home or hallway, for example, or (from a feng shui perspective) the 'wealth zone' of your house or apartment. Draw an infinity symbol on the cardboard, using two lines, one inside the other, to create a strip within which you can write – make sure it is wide enough to include everything you have in mind. Cut out the symbol shape and place it on the drawing paper as a template. Draw around the template with a pen or pencil and fill in the paper lemniscate, using words, paintings or drawings to denote all the things you would like in your life. Remember: this will be your personal lemniscate of infinite possibilities and endless potential for development. It may take a few days to complete; allow yourself time to reflect on what you would like to achieve.

You might like to listen to music while completing your lemniscate or to burn some soothing incense, or light a candle and invite your guardian angels to help. Just make sure you allow yourself enough time so that you don't feel rushed but are able to complete it in an atmosphere of relaxation and contentment. When you are happy with the results, cut out and glue the paper lemniscate to the cardboard template.

You can of course also activate the other side of the cardboard by adding a second paper lemniscate, with different hopes and desires. Laminate your lemniscate for extra protection and durability. Alternatively, if you have the necessary tools, you could make the symbol out of metal or wood. Attach or hang it in your chosen position; it represents the endless possibilities in your life and should be a constant reminder that your creative powers know no limits – they are infinite. You will have a very individual decoration with great potential for personal growth.

The balance between the two halves of the brain

The infinity symbol is used in a wide range of therapies to bring the two sides of our brains into balance. We feel good when both the rational and emotional parts of our brain interact perfectly and are in balance. Things to do with our feelings and emotions are dealt with by the right side, while the left side handles analytical thinking.

This situation is reversed in the body, however, where the left side is related to our feelings and female energy, and is controlled by the right half of the brain, while the right side of the body is subject to male, rational energy and is controlled by the left half of the brain. Throughout our lives, one side of the brain is more dominant than the other. In the West, where the emphasis is on learning, theory and use of the intellect, the education system often places greater emphasis on the stimulation of the left side of the brain. There is frequently little opportunity to put the right side of our brain to use in any positive or useful way, and indeed we may often fear our emotions. On the whole, we have not learned to accept our feelings as something useful or we fail to give them the appropriate attention. Feelings can be seen as an expression of weakness and so the focus

tends to be on over-developing the left, rational, materialistic side of our brains. In most countries the school system tends to promote this one-sided development strategy, and is proud of the fact. The neglect of the right side of the brain in education makes itself felt in unwelcome and detrimental ways, resulting in emotional coldness or indifference.

Similarly, accepting no responsibility for the well-being of our fellow human beings or feeling little or no empathy for the other creatures on this planet are also consequences of this one-sided focus on the brain. Fear of our emotions and suppressing the side of us that feels are also indicative of a strong emphasis being placed on the rational half of the brain. Many people are insecure as far as their feelings are concerned; they no longer know what or how they feel as they have never learned to rely on what they feel within themselves or to trust in the truth of these feelings. In fact, most of us have had the opposite experience – learning that it is painful and also undesirable to delve too deeply into our feelings. Many people in Western society, where the focus is on success, made a decision in childhood to ignore their feelings rather than trust in them.

We have been conditioned to approach life in a certain way, rationally, materialistically and selfishly, with the goals of performance, success and speed. The school system did not have – and still doesn't have – much interest in the creative forms of expression of the right half of the brain. In some countries, just a few 'alternative' schools, some offering certificates not recognised by governing bodies, focus on a holistic education, recognising the infinite capacities of human beings and offering a balanced education that promotes the development of both sides of the brain. People who fail to develop their emotive, creative right brain hemisphere are more easily led, sometimes believing that the material world is all there is.

Our understanding of magic is centred in the right side of our brains, not in the left. If we are conditioned only to recognise materialism, competition and mutual exploitation, the result is that we are more inclined to follow the herd. A personality that is too strongly aligned towards the left side of the brain leads to corruption, dishonesty, resentment, envy, hatred, fear and manipulation. If we could achieve wholeness and if both halves of the brain could be used in balance, there would be no more division and the dream of oneness through the acceptance of opposites could be realised on Earth. We would understand that the Earth looks after us all equally and that there is no sense in behaving arrogantly or manipulatively, as the only people we hurt by doing so are ourselves. By emphasising competition and the material side of life, we separate ourselves from the You that surrounds us, thereby standing in the way of our awakening and our path to enlightenment. Bringing the two sides of the brain into harmony requires both work and patience. You may have placed such a strong emphasis on the left side of your brain for many years that it will take some time to awaken the right side, the emotive, creative half of the brain from its Rip van Winkle-like slumber.

It is also important that the two halves of the brain can begin to work together and are allowed to be involved in expressing our lives and happiness. From now on, grant logic and emotion permission to work in tandem and take part in a mutual exchange of experiences and wisdom. Give yourself time to learn to trust your feelings and the creative expression of your life again. Let your judgemental attitude towards yourself and your progress (an attitude that stems from the left, rational half of the brain) slowly fade away to leave a loving and understanding approach to life in its wake. Never stop training the right half of your brain. Learn to trust the fact that your creative inspiration can also be useful.

Our brains can do so much more than we have been taught. To a large extent, our inventiveness and creative powers are due to the interplay between the two sides of our brain. Our completeness and health depend on their balanced co-existence, which is equally true for our brains. The heart centre we would like to use more actively and the heart voice we would like to hear more clearly are similarly connected to the right hemisphere of our brain, where the potential for recognising and expressing our emotions is located. Our brains are both our ingenuity HQ and our ally – if we can learn to use them to their full capacity, rather than just a part of them. When both sides of our brain are working in tandem, we will be able to enjoy the full expression of our lives.

There are various ways in which we can help to activate our left and right brain, such as music specifically composed to balance the two halves, available in any well-stocked music store, but one of the most effective is the infinity symbol. The most common types of therapy for harmonising the brain that can incorporate work with the infinity symbol are kinesiology and Brain Gym®. Even the more sceptical have established that the interaction of the two halves of the brain is boosted when both hands, crossed over the centre of the body, are used to trace a figure-of-eight. The various exercises that engage the vibrational frequency of the infinity symbol are used in particular with children challenged by a range of learning difficulties or impaired concentration. Balancing the two halves of the brain helps produce better coordination between thinking and feeling. For the two halves to work well together, it is important to get used to making movements that cross the centre of our bodies. The link between the left and right halves of the brain is encouraged through such physical exercises. Once we learn to bring the two sides of our brains into harmony and to use both equally, we will have a far wider range of ways of expressing ourselves, enabling us to live life to the full. When our logical and emotional sides work in harmony, we feel well mentally and physically; we make wise decisions and feel powerful, competent and full of life. We are more at ease socially and in

our everyday lives. We are more empathetic, not just with ourselves but with all other living creatures, and we become more resilient and better able to protect ourselves from life's intrusions. With the two halves of the brain in balance, we recognise when it is important to say 'yes', but equally learn when it is necessary to say 'no', striking a better balance with our innate desire to help others. We also feel more in control and stronger in terms of self-esteem and our positive assertiveness. We are able to make the most of our cognitive abilities, learning faster and more easily, and we are better able to retain what we have learned. We develop a greater ability to concentrate and boost our memory.

Excercises involving kinesiological balancing have achieved excellent success rates, especially with children, who are still in a very active phase of learning. I am not surprised that learning difficulties and attention deficit disorders are becoming increasingly identified in children in our Western education system in particular, but in adults, too. For some years now it has been clear that we need to find a new and balanced way of educating children. You could say that children are protesting through their behaviour, showing us that the current educational method is no longer acceptable – they need to be able to both think and feel. They are allowing our education systems to come crashing to the ground and they don't want to be forced to live in a society governed by the left side of the brain any more.

There is talk of a new golden age, of awakening, ascension, enlightenment, new dimensions; our children are wise old souls who have come in bodily form to show us this change in direction. No mention has been made of how easy this transition on Earth, of which we are a part, will be, nor of how soon it will happen – it is a question of mindfulness, patience, continuity and ongoing learning; of developing the truly altruistic and decent traits within us, such as love, empathy, harmony, balance, peace, acceptance, awareness, goodness of heart and all the good character attributes that we would like to see present in our lives. The eternally balancing flow of energy in the lemniscate is the symbol of awakening for us all. If we want to develop a healthy society for the future, we need to move away from an emphasis and focus upon just one side of the brain towards a new equilibrium and the freedom to use both sides in tandem once more. It is not a difficult concept but patience is needed to implement the change and put it into practice in our daily life, and in every moment of it. Distancing ourselves from a society with an exaggerated emphasis on performance is not easy, and our vanity, a trait seated in the left half of our brains, has received some thorough training over the last few decades.

Exercise:
Combining the two halves of the brain

Stand up straight. Allow your left hand to hang down beside your body in a relaxed way, and work with your right hand only. With the thumb pointing upwards, describe a large sideways figure-of-eight in the air in front of you with your right hand, making sure the crossing point of the two loops is in the centre of your body, at heart level. The two loops should be balanced and the same size. Extend your right hand as far to the left and right as you can without straining and keep your torso straight. Keeping your head still, follow the movement with your eyes. Now swap hands and carry out the same exercise with your left hand. Repeat the exercise for a couple of minutes, alternating hands.

For the more experienced

Arms outstretched, place one hand over the other in front of your chest at heart level. Use both hands together to describe a large sideways figure-of-eight in the air, going as far to the left as you can, keeping your body straight and remaining comfortable, and then making another loop to the right.

The loops of the figure-of-eight shape should always cross
at about the height of your chest. Keeping your body and
your head still, follow the movement with your eyes.

Make sure you breathe easily and deeply during the exercise. After a few minutes, you will feel calm and more at
ease deep within yourself. The left and right halves of your
brain are beginning to relax and form a better connection
with one another. Stress is relieved, allowing inner peace
to spread through you. By repeating the infinity symbol
movement, you are connecting the left and right halves of
the brain in a very simple and effective way; you will feel
more cheerful and alert. There is no need to concentrate
your thoughts in any particular direction while you carry
out the exercise – simply focus on the movement and
trust in the infinity symbol to work for your greatest good.
Carry out between 12 and 20 repetitions in one direction,
then change to the other direction for the same number
of repetitions.

TIP: This exercise will only take up a few minutes of your
time and it doesn't matter what time of day you do it. It
can be performed whenever you have a break in concentration, for example, or need a quick way to ground
yourself – just repeat several infinity symbol shapes in

front of your chest at heart level, as described. The only equipment you need is your hands so you can do this exercise anywhere and at any time.

Exercise: Conducting

This exercise is also for the more experienced but is simple to master. Once again, it starts with a movement in front of your chest, about level with your heart.

Move your left hand to the left while moving your right hand to the right and create an infinity symbol in the air with each hand, allowing the two shapes to cross at a point in the middle of your chest.

Repeat the movement for several minutes. It may feel rather like conducting a waltz! Do the exercise as many times as you like, or whenever you need to boost your concentration.

Exercise: Nose and ear

Using the fingers of your left hand, gently take hold of the tip of your nose while gently gripping your left ear with the fingers of your right hand; your right arm will be crossed over your left arm. Now simultaneously take your hands from the tip of your nose and your ear and swap the fingers of your right hand onto your nose and the fingers of your left hand onto your right ear. As you swap, your hands will describe a gentle sideways figure-of-eight in front of your face.

This exercise is good for your coordination and for improving the balance between the left and right sides of your brain. It will also help make you calmer and more centred. Once you can do the exercise accurately and well, try closing your eyes for a more meditative experience, and synchronise the hand movements with your breath. You will notice how your ability to concentrate increases.

Exercise: Elephant's trunk

Touch the tip of your nose with the fingers of your left hand. Now pass your right hand through the loop formed by your left arm. Extend your right arm through the hole and describe a figure-of-eight in the air with your right hand. Follow the movement with your eyes. After a couple of minutes, swap hands, touching the tip of your nose with the fingers of your right hand and using your left arm to draw the symbol in the air.

Tip: This is also an excellent exercise for children.

These exercises, which can be carried out in succession, provide a better way into the infinite creative potential within us, of which most of us use only a tiny fraction. It is not a question of being unwilling to use our creative potential, but rather that no one has ever shown us how to get the two sides of our brain working in unison, like a well-oiled machine. The infinity symbol offers endless possibilities to help us find a new direction for our whole being.

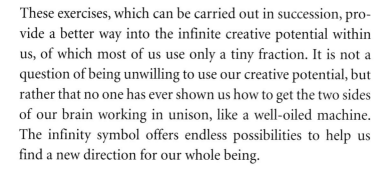

Living in duality and striving for harmony

Although the majority of people may well wish things were different, the fact is that we live in a dual world here on Earth. Our lives subsume day and night, light and dark, good and evil, hot and cold, male and female, light and heavy, yin and yang, above and below, feast and famine… and the very ability to differentiate between the two sides of a duality arises from a knowledge of such opposites; had we not encountered heat, we would have no word for cold. As soon as too much emphasis is placed on any one thing, however, it weakens the other, and the result is disharmony. Having too many sweet things makes us want something sour. Balancing duality is therefore the highest goal of our lives on Earth. It is only when we pay enough attention to the power inherent in balance that we have a chance of building a new paradise on Earth together.

We lightworkers are here on Earth to restore balance to the scales. We are the balance, one of the two loops in the figure-of-eight. For the lemniscate of the Earth to be returned to horizontal balance, we should focus our collective strength on our light, love, generosity, empathy, peace and unity. The time has come to use the energy of equilibrium, brought to

us by the infinity symbol, for our personal development and expansion of our consciousness.

Our efforts will help to create a new space for living on Earth, a place for our descendants. Past cultures have shown that placing too strong an emphasis on an either/or approach, where you have to choose one thing over another, ultimately leads to destruction. Disharmony was always the source of their downfall, while longevity arises from harmony and the interplay of dualities – in other words, from following a balanced middle path.

strength lies in balance

The principles of equilibrium and balance become apparent at the point when a lack is experienced or a fault noted – we seek to strike a balance and realise what we desire. When we enjoy an excess of something, however, we have no desire to balance it out, and may decline any offer or attempt to do so. We may become fearful since our tendency is to adopt one of two extremes instead of living in harmony. Most people think and follow a pattern of either/or alternatives, rather than striving for a harmonious not-only-but-also approach. I don't want to give the impression that I don't believe we should live in a land of plenty – far from it; it is simply a question of how we live in this abundance and whether we can also create space within it for its opposite, for emptiness.

Just as we can't have endless sunshine here on Earth or the natural world would dry out – rain and moisture are vital – so it is with all that surrounds us. We can relax, welcoming both the dry warmth of the sun and the cooling dampness of rain, embracing both joyfully. When we find unity within ourselves and learn to live our lives embracing it, we will be able to create new unity around us. Harmony and balance – both for ourselves and the environment – depend upon equalising interconnections and accepting dualities. We will achieve this in turn by understanding the true power behind the simple symbol of the lemniscate. The Earth is a planet of duality, and the more easily we come to terms with this, the better we will recognise and make use of the principles of duality within us, and the more rapidly we will progress along our path to wholeness or being at one.

Food for thought

Take a few moments to reflect on your everyday life. Think of an occasion when you had to make an important either/ or decision. Think back – how did it feel to have to make that choice and to choose just one option? Now think about those scenarios in your life that could be described as 'not-only-but-also'; be aware of how differently you feel about them deep inside. The either/or scenarios generally don't have much leeway for creative solutions and often make you feel ill at ease, while in contrast the not-only-but-also routes stimulate creativity, offering much more room to manoeuvre and so lead the centre within us towards balance. How is your life at the moment? How often do you put yourself under the same pressure rather than tune in to the vibration of the infinity symbol, which traces both sides in a harmonious circuit and creates new order in your life? Allow yourself to follow the middle path and liberate yourself from the paralysing energy of single-sidedness.

Exercise:
Free yourself from an either/or situation

Draw a large infinity symbol on a sheet of paper. Write down all the 'eithers' relating to a question you are trying to answer in one loop and all the 'ors' in the other. Trace along the line of the symbol with your pen several times until you feel a little more at ease in yourself. As you do so, imagine the two sides of the symbol embarking upon an energetic dance with one another as the paralysis of your thoughts dissolves in the vibrational energy and light of the lemniscate, and then begins to resonate. Listen intently to what is inside you and keep telling yourself that you are open to both options. Both possibilities are available and are not mutually exclusive. Over the next few days,

continue to trace the infinity symbol, until you feel a new ease in your innermost being – not necessarily related to either of the options, but simply offering leeway for an independent solution inspired by the illumination and increased vibrational frequency of the lemniscate.

Here is a typical 'either/or' situation as an example. Your question might be: 'Should I move into a particular new apartment that is great but very expensive? Or should I stay in my old flat, which no longer meets my requirements?' Write down all the plus points of the new flat inside one loop, and the plus points for the old one in the other, and trace around the shape of the symbol (as described above) for a couple of consecutive days, without burdening yourself with expectations or stress. You may find that a third option arises, neither the old flat nor the new one but a completely different choice that may have been under your nose all along but escaped your notice.

The infinity symbol relaxes, harmonises and restores balance. It helps us to find a way out of situations that have become stuck in a rut. It allows us to get in touch with both the inner wisdom of our masculine ability to get things done and our female intuition. It provides us with the greatest possible support for our harmonious existence in a world of duality.

It is the key to a deeper understanding of how we can reconcile opposites – our daily lives and our lives in general will become far more relaxed and joyful.

Harmonious relationships in the energy of the lemniscate

The ability to 'achieve happiness and harmony in my relationship' is a key issue in many people's lives, with very few exceptions – along with how to enjoy it long term. The infinity symbol can help us move towards a closer integration of the duality within us while also progressing towards a deeper harmony. This kind of sympathetic balance is created from an inner peace and a harmonious alignment of the self.

We are born into either a male or a female body, but we also carry the energy of the other gender within us. If we are born into a female body, it is important to acknowledge the Feminine as a strength and something to which we should aspire, and to view – and accept – the Masculine, which is also present within us, as a support and an aid to the Feminine. In our Western society, it is unfortunately often the case that girls tend to be educated to be strong like men, independent and capable of asserting themselves, while boys are educated to be accommodating, understanding and – in particular – emotional. This creates confusion within us – we live in the body of a particular gender and yet act as if the energetic characteristics of the other gender were far more

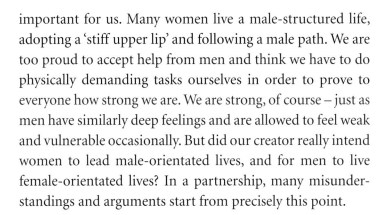

important for us. Many women live a male-structured life, adopting a 'stiff upper lip' and following a male path. We are too proud to accept help from men and think we have to do physically demanding tasks ourselves in order to prove to everyone how strong we are. We are strong, of course – just as men have similarly deep feelings and are allowed to feel weak and vulnerable occasionally. But did our creator really intend women to lead male-orientated lives, and for men to live female-orientated lives? In a partnership, many misunderstandings and arguments start from precisely this point.

If I was born into a female body, there was definitely a reason for it, and it is high time (if I have not already done so) for me to take my female side seriously. The male side is also inside me, but it is a foundation for my femininity, rather than the other way around. Exactly the same is true of men: the feminine and understanding side provides support for masculine assertiveness.

Participants in my seminars always laugh when I illustrate this with an example. Men would go out to hunt; they would kill a bear and then drag it back home with difficulty to their wives, who would then deal with turning the kill into food. The women made the home comfortable and looked after it with care. The men felt sustained and appreciated for their masculine strength when the women showed their pleasure at the success of the hunt. The women were aware of their value and felt equally important in their role. At this point, we might take a moment to think about how our everyday lives are in the West. Nowadays, most women go out themselves to kill the bear before dragging it laboriously home – only to be surprised that there is no one there to cook it. They are amazed at all the work needed to make the home comfortable and welcoming, and complain that they have to do everything themselves. Frustration about their lives, and their relationships in particular, is often the result.

Please don't misunderstand me here – I am not one of those people who say that women should get back in the kitchen. I simply think it is important that we all understand that both energies, male and female, exist on this Earth. Each is quite different and has different jobs to do. My concern is to respect both the masculine and the feminine side. It is important that each one of us can begin once again to assume the energy of our gender with mindfulness and love. It is my aim in this book to identify ways towards a solution along with new goals on which to focus in our development. The lemniscate is the key – it is the symbol that will help us to keep moving forward and progressing, and to unite all opposites in the most harmonious way possible. I am talking about mutual admiration and respect, authenticity and love, which can only be brought about by reconciling opposites. Wholeness arises from the harmonious combination of dualities. I have been born into a human body, but it took me some time to realise that I am the creator of many of the situations that I am not happy with: I analysed myself and my behaviour and realised that I was following a pretty male path. I was surprised that my partners would leave me, until I discovered that I was giving them no choice if they didn't want to be with a 'man' (from an 'energy' perspective).

My whole energy field and the way I conducted my daily life was very masculine, although my body is very feminine. Through my behaviour, I robbed my partners of any pleasure in being strong and masculine because I could do everything myself and, worse, I could do a lot of things better than they could and was even proud of the fact. So why would a man want to be in a relationship with me, if I didn't need (again, from an energy perspective) his protection, his strong hand and his masculinity? There was no yin and yang to form a whole in these relationships; there were two yangs in a kind of competition. The result was that my partners found other women who were glad to have a strong man at their side – women who were yin and were more than happy to form a whole unit with a yang. As you can imagine, it gave me food

for thought; I took a long hard look at myself and did some soul searching about what I believed in and what had shaped me, and I realised why I had such a tendency to be masculine. I associated the idea of femininity with concepts like 'weak', 'inadequate' and, even worse, with 'useless'. Because I didn't want to be those things, I went down a masculine route – even though I had been born into a female body.

After coming to this conclusion, I began to work on balancing out the masculine and feminine sides of me. I used the infinity symbol to help me find an appropriate harmony within myself. I understood what my really strong feminine attributes were and how they were helping my own masculine energy to assert this strong femininity. Although I was initially very unused to it and found it hard to show my tender, feminine side, it is now completely normal for me. I can honour and respect my feminine side and I have learned to keep the harmony between my masculine and feminine energy in balance. Once I had finally understood the creative interplay of the dual forces within me and had indeed begun to incorporate them into my life, I entered into a new and vital relationship; I was now able to acknowledge the masculine energy in my partner in a new way and could love myself as a woman with all my feminine strengths, and even enjoy them.

Men are not much better off, of course, as they are told early on in their education that it is important for them to show their feelings and that they have to be accommodating, which are typically female characteristics. They are discouraged from developing typically male traits with the energy of the 'warrior' and the 'hunter', and suppress their masculine strength in order not to be aggressive or assertive. At an early age, they learn to be conformist and loveable, against their own innate nature, which naturally does them little good. So many men find it difficult to deal with society's expectations, and have considerable problems with owning their masculinity with pride and joy. They carry within them confusion and uncertainty about what is expected of them as men, which has just the same corrosive effect on relationships as female confusion. The result is a man and a woman who want nothing more than to be happy with one another, but who are having a hard time finding their roles and allowing the happiness for which they are so desperate to appear in their lives.

The question raised in many of my seminars as well as in many individual consultations is this: How can I strengthen my femininity or masculinity and also learn to express it in my life? This is invariably a key question. In real-life relationships, the energy causing a blockage is often not being understood by your partner, or the fear of not being understood, or of having no opportunity to express your own needs or desires. Thanks to the power and insight that the infinity symbol brings, we can recognise the masculine and feminine qualities in our nature and the way in which we can bring ourselves into balance. The infinity symbol helps us to feel well again and to bring our own individual strength to a relationship. We can free ourselves from the learned patterns of behaviour that all too often result in separation rather than unification.

How can the infinity symbol help us with our partnerships and in our relationships in general?

The infinity symbol can be of great help in balancing our masculine and feminine strengths. The following exercises may look simple but are extremely effective. One of our basic human traits is to believe that things need to be difficult or challenging in order to benefit us and help us achieve success, so instead of following a path of continuity and ease, we tend to invest lots of effort and/or money in our development. We want to change ourselves but through external influences – however, the path of awakening to a fulfilled life is only possible when we make changes within and discover the energy of uniting oppositions.

Awakening is not to be found in struggle and strife. We should not feel we have to fight something within us, we simply have to find the path of enlightenment. Our aim is to understand duality in its deepest sense and to turn it into something we can use. True vital strength, which will help us along our path to awakening, is to be found through uniting the dualities that determine life on Earth. Only when we understand the dual powers within us and can embrace them in love – indeed, only when we acknowledge the balance and the equal value of everything that is polarised within us and around us – will we have an opportunity to immerse ourselves in our inner peace and unconditional love. The new society, the new Golden Age, the power of Aquarius lies in this understanding of the dual laws of the Earth and in balancing and linking all oppositions.

Exercise: Bringing the masculine and feminine sides within us into balance

You will need a large sheet of paper and a selection of different coloured pens. Draw an infinity symbol on the piece of paper. In one of the loops, write down all your masculine traits and in the other, all your feminine characteristics. Make sure that the descriptions are positive. Keep tracing the eight with the different pens, combining both male and female energies and with an attitude of respect within yourself; you are accepting both energies, and with every circuit, the dual flows of energy will be balanced and united harmoniously.

Exercise:
Bringing harmony to your relationship

Visualise the infinity symbol in your mind's eye. Now imagine yourself in one loop and your partner in the other. Mentally trace the line of the lemniscate over and over again until you perceive a harmonious, balanced energy within you. This simple exercise works particularly well when there is tension within the relationship. It leaves you space for your individuality while also leaving your partner room for the things that are unique to him or her. Try it out straight away. The exercise reduces tension and helps resolve differences of opinion in a more relaxed way. The constantly growing forces that unite us are encouraged in a very positive way, while the things that divide us are viewed in a deeply sympathetic way – as no longer so painful or negative. The infinity symbol provides space for our individuality and commonality simultaneously.

We often become aware of a wonderful, easy space between our partner and ourselves once we allow the infinity symbol to circulate and surround us as a vibrational frequency. As a result, we have more leeway to find creative solutions. Your partner does not have to be present, as this exercise will take effect across space and time.

Tip: You can do this exercise for anyone who is important to you, including siblings and parents, work colleagues, neighbours or managers. It is a positive and unifying route towards enabling more leeway and freedom for creative and positive solutions. It is one of my favourite exercises.

Exercise: Help in finding solutions

This exercise is effective for relationship problems and other issues. Visualise a large lemniscate, either in your home or perehaps while you are out in the countryside. In your mind's eye, begin to stroll along the figure-of-eight, taking it slowly, as it can take time for the solution to emerge from within you. Take the question with you from the positive pole of the lemniscate, through the neutral centre, to the negative pole and then back again.

This movement, this conscious awareness of the polarities and your simultaneous concentration on the question will create a new take on the situation, from which will arise a readiness for acceptance; and from this acceptance, a change will slowly develop that in turn will encompass a simplification of the issue. Calmly tracing the infinity symbol in our thoughts, again and again, helps us to reach the core of the issue and for the solution to present itself in a very simple way.

Tip: This is another of my favourite exercises, and I have had lots of positive feedback about it. The exercise is as simple as it is effective, and requires only a little patience and time. Distracted by focusing on walking and thinking about the question at the same time allows clarity to come forth from deep within us with greater ease. We don't get bogged down in scrabbling around for a potential answer, we just concentrate on walking – and an answer becomes apparent within ourselves. The exercise can be repeated as many times as required until things become quite clear and all questions have been answered.

Ritual: Attracting the ideal partner or creating more common ground in an existing relationship

You will need something like string (ideally a length of red cord or red wool), a large sheet of paper in pink or a shade of red, and two small photos, one of yourself and one of your partner. If you don't have a partner at the moment, use a photo of the person you would like to have as a part of your life. If you don't have a photo, write the name and date of birth of the person on the sheet of paper. If you have no idea who may be entering your life, write on the paper: 'I would like to share my life with the partner who suits me best, a partner with whom I form a whole unit and with whom I can exist in harmony. THANK YOU.' You may also like to jot down on the paper the characteristics you consider particularly important in your new partner.

Now make an infinity symbol with the red string, ideally somewhere that is special to you in your personal space. It might be a small house altar, a place for your angels, or the place where you always have fresh flowers and candle-light. Place your photo in one of the loops of the red infinity symbol and the photo of your partner (or the personal details/description of the partner you wish to invite into your life, written on the sheet of paper) in the other loop. Leave the two loops containing this personal data alone for the next couple of days. The lemniscate symbolises 'being at one', and through this ritual, you will be drawing unity or wholeness into your relationship or your future relationship. You will be opening up space for completely new opportunities in your relationship as you experience it, a chance for oneness, freedom and individuality, with a real sense of belonging together. It will all happen in a relaxed and harmonious way at an energetic level as a result of placing the photographs and information in the loops of the lemnsicate and in so doing surrounding them with this powerful symbol.

At this point, I would like to remind you that it is important for us to develop the virtue of patience. We humans tend to want everything we imagine and dream about to be available instantly; but the universe is not always minded to react straight away. It sometimes takes a while for the vibrational frequency of our energetic fields to balance out sufficiently for the miracles or changes we are expecting to be able to actually come about. Remind yourself how many years you have spent in one or another states of imbalance, and give yourself a chance to equalise the scales of your life over an appropriate period of time. Don't ask too much of yourself by being impatient and getting in the way of the success of your new-found insights. The path of change generally begins in our outermost energetic layers and then migrates through each of the seven layers, being integrated into each in turn. The material layer is the last in which integration takes place – so it is not surprising that many of the insights we achieve take time to manifest themselves on a physical level in our day-to-day lives.

An ancient Celtic wedding ritual

While I was writing about the infinity symbol and the connection between masculine and feminine and the way they are combined in our relationships, a married couple got in touch to ask if I would hold a ceremony for them – they wanted to renew their marriage vows on their 20th wedding anniversary, and they wanted to do so in a Celtic ceremony, surrounded by Nature at a place of power. It should come as no surprise to learn that the lemniscate is an important element of a very old heathen wedding ritual.

Couples who make or renew a promise to one another are joined by a priest in a handfasting ceremony. The couple stand facing one another, each placing their right hand in their partner's right hand and their left in their partner's left. This creates a figure of eight between the two; even in ancient times, this was a symbol of an endless connection. The priest wraps a cloth or cord that has been blessed around their hands before blessing the relationship and asking each to make their marriage vows. They either make a vow to share their lives as long as love endures (and should love no longer flow, for whatever reason, both partners have the option to dissolve their bond in a ceremony, and go their separate ways) or vow to share their lives for eternity. Such a vow endures until death and beyond.

The cord is then untied; the couple take it home and keep it safe on their house altar. A candle is also lit during the ceremony and brought back to the family home; it will be lit again during the good times and any challenging periods that their life together may bring. In such moments, the light of the candle is a reminder of the couple's shared vows and that, together, they will always have a solution and a light on the horizon. The ceremony also includes a shared drink of blessed water from a chalice, and the couple step over a broom together to symbolize entering their new life. Every action during the ceremony is sustained by the profound knowledge attained by the initiates who followed this path many centuries ago. This wedding ritual was abandoned only during the period of Christianisation and is now being carried out once more by people on a path to spiritual awakening. The ritual is not, of course, recognised officially and

is thus only suitable for those who have no desire for an offi-
cial marriage certificate or who wish to celebrate their lives
together a second time.

It was so wonderful to be asked to conduct this ritual just at
that very moment in time – these are always the magic signs
and portents along my path that make my heart sing with
joy and show me the ineffable wisdom of the creator Source.
I could never have planned it that way, and I would like to
thank those two dear people for their trust in me – thank you
for choosing absolutely the most fitting moment to approach
me with your request; your timing was simply impeccable.

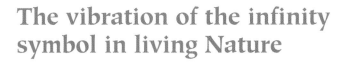

The vibration of the infinity symbol in living Nature

Water is one of the most vital things for us humans, and since we consist of more than 70 per cent water ourselves, it is no wonder that it is key to our survival. Water can be viewed on a par with consciousness; it is not of earthly origin and it is impossible to prove scientifically where our water originally came from. Water stores information and releases it in homeopathic doses. Several renowned water researchers have devoted their lives to understanding it – studying water molecules, aquatic structures and the pathways of water.

Someone who impressed me greatly, and whose findings I consider extremely helpful, is Austrian naturalist, philosopher and inventor Viktor Schauberger. He drew wisdom from the observation of water as it flows naturally, spending many hours in the natural world monitoring the links between free-flowing water, its natural powers of purification and its physical force. The knowledge gained from many years of observation resulted in a number of very useful ways to ener-gise water, such as the water swirler, which simulates the meandering movement of water in streams, rivers, torrents, natural lakes and ponds. Water traces an infinity symbol when it flows along the bed of a stream. Watch how water moves naturally and observe the currents and the amazing shapes it creates. This action purifies, balances and positively charges the water. Viktor Schauberger's water swirler, which can be positioned in a stream, comprises several basins that allow the water flowing through them to trace horizontally aligned figures-of-eight. The figures-of-eight form in the bowls, which are arranged along a slight slope, each bowl beneath the next. The water flows through a small hole into the first bowl and makes a figure-of-eight there before flowing down into the next bowl. The water moves from bowl to bowl, being enhanced with the vibrational energy of the infinity symbol in each, and is thus purified and revitalised.

For me, it was wonderful to find confirmation of the perfect effects of the lemniscate in running water. It underscores the absolute importance of this simple symbol. To enrich tap or drinking water with the energy of the infinity symbol, if you have no other means at your disposal, just trace the figure-of-eight shape on the surface of the water with a finger or use a stick, spoon or crystal wand. Simply dangling your hand in a bath full of water and making a figure-of-eight shape can be really pleasurable. Dip your hand into the water and keep tracing an infinity symbol across the whole surface. The water will be enhanced with the energy of the lemniscate.

Now you can enjoy a harmonising and relaxing bath. You can also make a figure-of-eight shape in a glass of water with a spoon, although it is enjoyable and beneficial to energise the water using a crystal wand since you will retain the vibrations of the precious stone in the water. Alternatively, you could have the infinity symbol engraved or attached as a sticker on the base of your water jug or glass. An energy tray featuring the symbol, on which you place the water jug or your food, can also be a great help. As we consist of such a high percentage of water, our internal water naturally reacts to energisation created with a crystal wand using the vibrational frequency of the infinity symbol. When choosing a crystal wand, take into account what the various stones represent in order to choose one to suit the issues that you want the crystal to balance out. If you are concerned about your solar plexus, for example, or have a constant tightness and tension in the area of your stomach, pick a crystal associated with the solar plexus chakra. Trace an infinity symbol in one direction on your skin at the solar plexus chakra for a few minutes, then change to tracing it in the other direction. You will

notice how the area slowly relaxes. The acupuncture points on the feet, hands and ear can also be calmed or balanced out with small infinity symbols. Trace figures-of-eight across your skin at the acupuncture points using the crystal wand. If you do not have a crystal wand, use your finger or an acupressure roller. This is a way of bringing either an excess or lack of energy into equilibrium. The infinity symbol will have a balancing effect each time – it will discharge if there is too much and top up if there is too little. Tense parts of the body or blocked energy can be brought back into new balance by working with the lemniscate.

Exercise: A balancing exercise for the body with a partner

You can do this exercise with your partner or a friend. One of you lies comfortably on your back on a massage table or a floor mat, covered with a throw or large towel to keep your body warm during the exercise. Create an atmosphere of well-being and relaxation; take time to prepare the room, which should radiate a clear, pure energy. Spritz a little room spray to purify or protect the room, for example, or prepare the space by burning some incense or joss sticks. Do what you can to avoid being disturbed. Set the mood for your exercise – the lighting and room temperature, and your inner attitude, all play a part.

When you first begin to balance your energy with the infinity symbol, take a few deep breaths so you are calm and entirely in the moment. Place your hands on your partner's ankles lying in front of you. Visualise the energy of the infinity symbol flowing from one palm to the other and thus balancing out the two ankles. Ankles represent being present in life. After a couple of minutes, gently take your hands from the ankles and lay them on your partner's knees. Once again, imagine the infinity symbol forming between your two hands, and the energy flowing. The knees represent humility and gratitude for our lives. After a few more minutes, remove your hands from your partner's knees and place them on the hips. Visualise the infinity symbol as you leave your hands motionless on the hip-bones. The hips and sacral region represent all the patterns we have been taught and all the partners with whom we have ever been in physical union. Issues relating to our parents, siblings and ancestors are also located in the sacral chakra.

Now remove your palms from the hips and place your hands gently on the lower ribcage, about level with the solar plexus. Once again, allow the infinity symbol to flow as a vibrational pattern between your palms. All our fears are stored in the solar plexus chakra. Even if we tend to overthink things, this will have a relaxing effect on our solar plexus region. After a short while, remove your hands from the ribcage and place them to the right and left of the chest, around the heart chakra. Once again, visualise a lemniscate between your palms. All our feelings are stored in our hearts, and it is here that we will get to grips with the big issues, such as love, unrequited love, rejection and everything we ourselves associate with such topics. Courage for a new beginning and great changes of every kind in our lives are also located in the heart chakra.

After several minutes of balancing, place your hands on your partner's shoulders. All the burdens that we pile upon ourselves are balanced out with the lemniscate. Everything that has ever weighed us down or oppressed us will undergo an alignment that brings it into equilibrium.

Now place your hands to either side of the hinge of the jaw and let the infinity symbol flow between your palms once again. This is where all the tension from difficult or impossible experiences collects, times when we had to bite our tongues and put on a brave face. This balancing helps us to let go and treat ourselves with more love and grace. Finally, place your hands on your partner's temples and let the energy of the infinity symbol flow through this

area of the head. This brings equilibrium to every issue that is currently troublesome, balancing the eyes and thus the sensitive windows to the soul.

Now gently remove your hands from your partner's energy field and give him or her a little time to return completely to the here and now. Compare notes on what you have just experienced, if you like, or just be aware that a great balancing, harmonisation and levelling out has been brought about with your hands, and through visualising the infinity symbol. You can now swap positions and experience the beneficial and harmonising vibrations of the lemniscate in your own energy field, chakras, emotional body and your whole being. This exercise takes a while to complete and requires a certain amount of concentration, so only do it when you have enough free time.

Tip: You can carry out this balancing exercise with your own hands on your own body; however, it is not quite as relaxing, as inevitably you can't work in quite the same way and might be too easily distracted by thinking about how to do the next part of the exercise.

The infinity symbol in the animal kingdom

In this chapter, I would like to look more closely at two groups of animals in particular, although I have no doubt there are plenty of other creatures that make use of the infinity symbol in one form or another.

Bees

Most people now understand just how important bees are for us all; if it weren't for these wonderful creatures, our natural world would soon become barren. By being responsible for the pollination of many plants and therefore those plants' continued existence, bees are hugely important – not to mention also for the wonderfully healthy products that bees produce that we humans enjoy. Bees live in highly social colonies in which every bee knows its exact position in the hierarchy of the hive from the moment it is hatched to its last breath, fulfilling its role without exception. It is fascinating to learn how honey bee foragers fly out in search of suitable places to feed before returning to the hive and performing a 'waggle dance'. Their task is to inform the bees back in the hive of the location of a good food source; as they perform

the dance, the bees move back and forth in a figure-of-eight to transmit to their fellow pollen collectors the exact coordinates of their discovery.

It is absolutely amazing – the waggle dance pinpoints the location so precisely that all the bees are able to find the site with ease. In the dance, the infinity symbol acts as a map showing the exact distances and directions in which the bees should fly, giving those in the hive about to head off precise information about the location of the feeding site, along with information about its size and how far away it is.

I don't know about you, but I think it's pretty impressive that highly organised bee colonies make use of this ancient symbol of perfect harmony. The bees also show us how it is possible to live with one another in harmony, forming a comunity and working together to achieve a common goal. For me, the bee also represents the concept of 'service', a concept that is not always popular with humans; each individual bee serves the greater whole, the higher good of the whole colony, to which everything else is subservient.

How fantastic it would be if we humans had a better understanding of our greater goal and could learn to love the admirable concept of 'service' too, by which I don't mean 'being a servant' but rather the all-encompassing, profound understanding that we are all here to further a greater or higher plan. What we generally perceive is only a tiny fraction of the wider design, so it is our job to trust that through our service for the good of the world, we can make the world into what in truth it really is – a paradise created from the harmonious integration of dualities. This paradise reveals itself to us in eternal, harmonious balance. The key preconditions for realising this paradise are the positive energies of trust, service and unconditional love in our earthly existence.

Birds

Birds symbolically represent the fire in our hearts. I was thrilled to discover that some birds (such as the humming-bird) are continuously tracing a figure-of-eight loop in the air as they fly. There are generally two mechanisms involved in bird flight (simplifying it greatly): lift and forward motion. In so-called 'flapping flight', the wings trace a figure-of-eight shape. If you can combine the fire of your heart and the harmoniously balancing energetic vibrations of the infinity symbols, you will perhaps also understand what these creatures are doing for us all; as they fly, these birds are continually bringing balance to the world, providing every other

living creature – including humans, of course – with the energetic vibrations of the infinity symbol via the energetic field that surrounds us. They harmonise, balance and help us to reconcile oppositions into a new order of peaceful coexistence. So you could simply look at it like this: the more birds we have around us, the greater the chances of balance and harmony.

The 'figure-of-eight' within us

It's at this point that I'm reminded of a story I read years ago that moves me today as much as it did then. It opened up the path to myself and my innermost treasures. It told of how our creator was unsure of exactly where he should place the highest wisdom for all those who decide to seek perfection. It was important that each person who was truly seeking this wisdom – no matter what their age – should be able to find it.

After choosing and then rejecting several places on Earth, the creator Source decided to choose a place very close to us – indeed, within us – in our very cells, our hearts, our essence. Everything we need to follow our path to enlightenment, everything that might help us to achieve true awakening, lies within us.

Observing the stages of cell division after fertilisation through a microscope, we can see that the infinity symbol occurs here, too. So even right at the very beginning of our lives there is already an indication that here on Earth, we are entering a world of duality; and the infinite, balancing vibrational frequency inherent in the unity of all dual circumstances will lead to true wholeness and all-encompassing

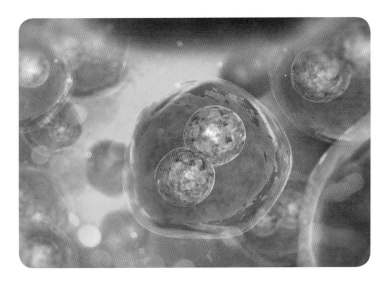

completeness. New life is created from the integration and unification of two cells, an egg and a sperm.

It is not just the first division of cells that reminds us of the energy of the figure-of-eight vibrations within us, however. The figure-of-eight is deeply embedded in our cells, in the basic structure of our genes. It is found in a repeating arrangement in the double helix construction of our DNA strands, and here, too, we encounter the numerological code 'GOD'. If you would like to find out more about this, I can recommend the book *The God Code: The Secret of our Past, the Promise of our Future* by Gregg Braden. So we carry the blueprint for finding the path back to unity, to the creator Source, within our own cells – close at hand and accessible in an instant. This is the single moment in which we dare to take the ultimately decisive step and seek for the truth within us rather than outside us – the all-encompassing universal truth that leads to our awakening, the truth that was stored by the wise creator Source within us, the truth that is always available and accessible in an instant.

The figure-of-eight shape is also found in the basic structure of proteins, as well as in collagen fibres. For me, these are all indications that we always carry the greatest wisdom within ourselves. We have just forgotten that everything is already within us and that we are free to learn how to decode this important information in our human incarnation. The eternal balancing energy of the lemniscate already resides inside us and connects our being with the cosmic flow, with the Source from which we originate. Our genetic code bears within it an opportunity to recognise this. If we are the incarnation of duality on this planet, our goal is to recognise the eternal balance of all polarising forces. Instead of fighting the dual powers that affect us, our true concern is to achieve new acceptance and the peaceful equilibrium of this duality.

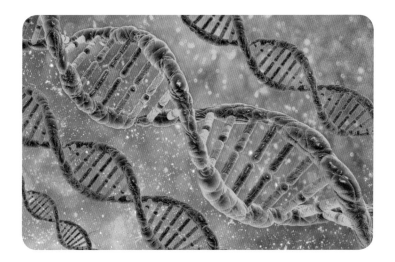

The code for our path back to unity is therefore not to be found outside but inside us, stored within our cells. If we want to achieve awakening and become aware, observing consciously and with mindfulness, we have many opportunities to do so. All the wise ones who trod the path of awakening before us left signs that will help us find the path to acceptance of the rules of earthly existence more easily.

By learning to balance out duality and bring it into our own harmony, we gain the independence that we want so desperately for ourselves. In the infinity symbol, we have been given a powerful instrument and when we understand that our redemption lies in duality rather than in judging others or clinging on to any one thing, a field of harmony, peace and unconditional love will be created within us and around us, as if by itself. The infinity symbol reminds us that our life is in constant flux, an eternal path of development from the positive to the negative pole. The only constant from the moment of our birth to the moment of our passing is change, perpetual motion. If we apply this insight to our lives, it becomes perfectly clear that our development here on Earth will never be complete.

As long as we inhabit a human body, we are subject to the laws of duality and thus to the immutable necessity of balancing this duality in a harmonious way. Our principal goal should be to understand this duality deep within us – not just in our minds, but in every single cell. We should work tirelessly, with every breath in our body, towards recreating a harmonious balance and making use of this insight on our path towards perfection. In its quiet and unassuming way, the lemniscate shows us the comprehensive wisdom of the creator's greatest plan and how we can contrive to follow it. It functions as a metaphor for the human path to development and decision-making. The infinity symbol represents the transformation of matter into pure vibrational energy.

Tips and exercises for working with the lemniscate

The symbolic power of the infinity symbol can be used to bring together everything that you wish to unite in harmony. You can do this anywhere you like, simply by using your mind and visualising yourself in one of the two loops and in the other, the person or event that is worrying or troubling you or that you simply wish to embrace in greater harmony. Now trace this figure-of-eight repeatedly in your mind until you feel that everything has been balanced out, or any troubling emotions or thoughts that have been stirred up have been quietened, or until you simply feel better.

This technique really can be used for anything you want to harmonise and bring into balance, as often as you feel is necessary and right. As it means you are working to bring balance, rather than to intervene, you will not be burdening yourself with karma of any kind whatever. If you carry out this exercise for other people (i.e. you are not one of the subjects), it is important not to impose any dominant wish or intention on the lemniscate; simply ask for the greatest possible harmony for all concerned.

Try it out – for your children, for example. Place a person – Try it out – for your children, for example. Place a person – such as a teacher with whom your child doesn't get on so well – in one loop and your child in the other. Or try the exercise with one of your child's playmates with whom there should be greater harmony or balance, visualising an infinity symbol and energetically placing your child in one of the loops and the playmate in the other. Think back to the first exercise at the beginning of the book (see page 4). Do this exercise again – but in your mind. Let the energy flow continuously along the path of the infinity symbol, first in one direction and then in the other. Repeat the energetic exercise as many times as necessary until you notice a marked improvement in the situation. Even after a much greater harmony has been created, continue supporting your child with this exercise at least once a week.

You can also provide support for your loved ones by visual-ising them with their line manager, for example, inside the different loops of an infinity symbol and then tracing along its lines again and again in your mind. You don't have to mention what you are doing, just follow the exercise and share your partner's joy when the tension in the difficult situation they are experiencing eases and your loved one and their manager start to work together harmoniously. You could also do the exercise to support your colleagues or

neighbours who aren't getting on well. It is all about making what separates people more understandable and providing a balance in the energetic field. You are not interfering as long as you don't allow any of your own desires or preconceived goals to flow into the vibrations of the figure-of-eight; you are merely opening up the energy field for balance and harmony. This is just one of the wonderful opportunities afforded by lightwork.

You could paint a lemniscate directly onto your skin or draw one on a sticker and place it on your skin. Try attaching the infinity symbol to points on your body where you need harmonisation. It can also be painted on the skin to help with pain, breaks, tension, sprains and any other imbalance in the body. Use body paint to draw a single lemniscate, or two or three that overlap, on the affected area. The lemniscate can also be used to help speed up the healing of wounds. However, never paint directly onto an open wound, but instead draw the symbol around the wound at an appropriate distance from it, or above or below the wound or any plaster or bandage covering it. Use the uniting and harmonising symbol of the lemniscate as often as feels right for you. It has worked really well for me.

The harmonising infinity symbol can also be used for pets – draw it on your pet's bed or food bowl, or once again visualise a figure-of-eight, with your pet in one of the loops and yourself in the other, to harmonise your relationship with them or make your bond closer. If your pet is injured, the

infinity symbol can be used to help speed up the healing process. The method is the same as for humans: draw the lemniscate up to three times near or around the injured area (but not on an open wound). If you are working with a cat, draw the lemniscate in their energy field, as cats dislike their fur being disrupted against the direction of growth and it will only irritate them more and excite them unnecessarily. However, if you want to introduce the infinity symbol into their energy field with a repeated stroking motion, your cat will find it very calming and it will help the healing process.

If a plant is not thriving, draw the lemniscate on its container or on the watering can that you use for it. Or just draw an infinity symbol on the tap you use to fill your watering can or attach a sticker bearing the symbol to it. Using your fingers or a stick, trace a figure-of-eight in the surface of the water you are about to pour onto your plants. It will help keep your plants healthy and reward you with thick foliage and flowers. Use the power of the infinity symbol every evening before going to sleep by drawing a big double-loop in the air above your bed or that of your child. It can have a calming effect on anyone experiencing difficulty sleeping. Draw a large lemniscate on the floor and stand inside it with one foot in each loop, positioning your body above the centre point. Close your eyes and visualise the infinity symbol rising upwards.

Imagine the symbol moving up from your feet, climbing up your legs to your hips and your back, then to your chest and over your head, bringing everything within you and in your energy field into the eternal, harmonious balancing vibration of the lemniscate. This exercise will align your centre line and strengthen your core energy, while the left and right halves of your body and all your organs will undergo a harmonious connection with one another. The lemniscate will rise up to the original Source and connect you in a harmonious energy field with your creator and all the beings in heaven – all the angels, archangels, elohim, seraphim, Light Beings and Ascended Masters will join you in this harmonious vibration. Then visualise the lemniscate returning to a horizontal position and swinging down to the heart of Mother Earth, bringing you as a human being into a harmonious connection with the planet, the natural world and every living thing. You are a conduit between heaven and Earth and a unifying part of an infinite vibrational frequency of peace and love. Let this string of figures-of-eight flow through your body from top to bottom for a while, enjoying the balancing vibration and feeling how your chakras and all your cells are charged up with these harmonious vibrations.

When outside in the natural world, try to walk in a figure-of-eight shape as often as possible. Consider your starting point and final destination and plan how you can choose a path that will follow the figure-of-eight shape. Alternatively, walk in lots of small figures-of-eight as you make your way along the path. It is geat fun to make figures-of-eight as you walk in snow or on sand, and you might even be able to get your children to join in and get excited about it, too. If you have a garden, planting flowers or bushes in a figure-of-eight shape looks attractive and, from an energetic point of view, is also extremely beneficial – both for you and for your environment. Arranging pretty stones in the shape of an infinity symbol will also produce a wonderful effect. You could even draw the symbol in the sand of a Zen garden.

Final thoughts

Be creative and use the infinity symbol wherever and however you can. Give free rein to your desire to achieve balance and harmony. The great thing about working with the lemniscate is that it costs nothing and that this powerful symbol is always there at your fingertips, ready to be used in the simplest of ways – so do make use of it as often as possible, and enjoy bringing harmony to everything.

You can view this as part of your duties as a lightworker. Even if those around you are not conscious or aware of it and you receive no thanks, you will be changing the world. Think of the butterfly effect: the flap of a butterfly's wing can cause a tornado. Acknowledge what you are doing, respect yourself and your love for every living creature, and remain constant on your path of development and change.

The lemniscate is a symbol representing infinity, eternal development and balance; it describes the absolute, and in itself is an expression of unity, wholeness and completeness. The more often it is used in our day-to-day lives, the better things will be for us and for every living thing. We all want to restore paradise on Earth, which is why it is so important that we work tirelessly towards change, bringing about balance, harmony, and an understanding of the laws of duality, unconditional love and peace.

Even if success is not immediate, trust that the beat of your wings has achieved something great and that, through your tireless lightwork, you are involved in changing the world.

Begin by harmonising yourself, immersing yourself in the wholeness to be discovered in the equilibrium of duality. Use the wisdom of the lemniscate and become the perfect being that you were at birth. The world will change as you pass on this simple wisdom. I know that bringing about wholeness

and understanding duality, not to mention accepting and integrating them, will not always be easy, but it can be fun. And if you don't get the ball rolling, who else will?

I wish you many harmonious moments in the energy of the lemniscate and wherever you go, always remember how powerful this simple symbol is and use it as often as you can; you will not only be supporting your own awakening, you will be giving the gift of infinity to others.

About the author

Barbara Heider-Rauter is a qualified educator and therapist with years of practical experience. In her seminars and training courses she considers it her role to act as a clear and loving guide for all true seekers. The deep insights she has attained into spiritual interconnections and unseen worlds allow her to recognise the uniqueness of every individual and perceive their alignment with the light within. She is also a leading Aura-Soma expert and a teacher of this wonderful colour system. Her work has always been oriented towards the greatest developmental potential and well-being of each individual. She leads meditation evenings and seminars on personal development and undertakes seminar trips to Britain (to visit the mystical places from the King Arthur legends) and 'heart journeys' to Ireland. For more than 15 years she has run a specialist spiritual shop in Salzburg, Austria, that provides a meeting place for kindred spirits and all those who seek.

www.avalon-spirit.com
www.barbara-heider-rauter.com

Picture credits

Picture on p. 101 (bees): © Roland Rauter

Decorative designs: majcot: background, GONHIN: background and payapple: infinity symbol. All shutterstock.com.

Both Ho'oponopono, the Hawaiian forgiveness ritual, and family constellation therapy help to heal our relationships with the world around us and bring healing to our inner world. This hands-on book brings together what belongs together, providing beginners with an introduction and easy access and the more experience with fresh insights.

Ulrich Emil Duprée
Ho'oponopono and Family Constellations
A traditional Hawaiian healing method for
relationships, forgiveness and love
Paperback, full colour throughout, 160 pages
ISBN 978-1-84409-717-3

Powerful yet concise, this revolutionary guide summarizes the Hawaiian ritual of forgiveness and offers methods for immediately creating positive effects in everyday life. Ho'oponopono consists of four consequent magic sentences: 'I am sorry. Please forgive me. I love you. Thank you.' By addressing issues using these simple sentences we get to own our feelings, and accept unconditional love, so that unhealthy situations transform into favorable experiences.

Ulrich Emil Duprée
Ho'oponopono
the Hawaiian forgiveness ritual as the key
to your life's fulfilment
Paperback, full colour throughout, 96 pages
ISBN 978-1-84409-597-1

EARTHDANCER

The Miracle Problem-Solver provides the key to solving every problematic situation in your life, quite literally in a stone's throw. This book is for all those wanting to connect to universal wisdom and heal their lives in a few simple steps. The solution lies within the problem!

Kira Klenke
The Miracle Problem-Solver
Using crystals and the power of Sedona
to transform your life
Paperback, full colour throughout, 96 pages
ISBN 978-1-84409-698-5

This powerful book with its beautiful dragon illustrations allows you to enter the mystical world of dragons. Once you are ready, it will help you to get to know your own dragon, your close personal companion, and to share its invincibility, wisdom and magic.

Christine Arana Fader
The Little Book of Dragons
Finding your spirit guide
Paperback, full colour throughout, 120 pages
ISBN 978-1-84409-670-1

This is an easy-to-use A-Z guide for treating many common ailments and illnesses with the help of crystal therapy. It includes a comprehensive colour appendix with photographs and short descriptions of each gemstone recommended.

Michael Gienger
Healing Crystals
the A–Z guide to 555 gemstones, 2nd edition
Paperback, full colour throughout, 128 pages
ISBN 978-1-84409-647-3

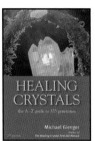

Adding crystals to water is both visually appealing and healthy. It is a known fact that water carries mineral information and Gem Water provides effective remedies, acting quickly on a physical level. It is similar and complementary to wearing crystals, but the effects are not necessarily the same.

Gem Water needs to be prepared and applied with care; this book explains everything you need to know to get started!

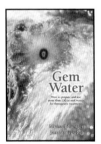

Michael Gienger, Joachim Goebel
Gem Water
How to prepare and use more than
130 crystal waters for therapeutic treatments
Paperback, full colour throughout 96 pages
ISBN 978-1-84409-131-7

This useful little guidebook provides everything you need to know about cleansing crystals – both the well-known and the less well-known methods – clearly explaining which method is best for each purpose, whether for discharging or charging, cleansing on an external or energetic level, or eliminating foreign information.

Michael Gienger
Purifying Crystals
How to clear, charge and purify
your healing crystals
Paperback, full colour throughout, 64 pages
ISBN 978-1-84409-147-8

This pocket pharmacy of healing stones embraces many applications. Although describing only twelve stones, the breadth of its scope resembles a home pharmacy. From allergies to toothache, you will find the right stone for every application. This handy little book offers you the essence of our modern knowledge of healing stones.

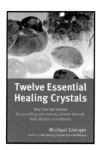

Michael Gienger
Twelve Essential Healing Crystals
Your first aid manual for preventing
and treating common ailments
from allergies to toothache
Paperback, full colour throughout, 64 pages
ISBN 978-1-84409-642-8

For further information and to request a book catalogue contact:

Inner Traditions, One Park Street, Rochester, Vermont 05767

Earthdancer Books is an Inner Traditions imprint.

Phone: +1-800-246-8648, customerservice@innertraditions.com

www.earthdancerbooks.com • www.innertraditions.com

EARTHDANCER

AN INNER TRADITIONS IMPRINT